Pathway to Purpose

A Path for Teens to Real World Success

Pathway to Purpose

A Path for Teens to Real World Success

Jeff Yalden, CSP

Pathway to Purpose
A Path for Teens to Real World Success

Jeff Yalden, CSP

Published by: YALDEN PRESS PUBLISHING
PO Box 541
Greenville, NH 03048

Phone: 800-948-9289
Email: jeff@jeffyalden.com
Web: www.jeffyalden.com

Cover design and layout: Ad Graphics, Inc.
Printed in the United States of America

ISBN: 0-9747482-0-X

Warning – Disclaimer
The purpose of this book is to educate and entertain. The author or publisher does not guarantee that anyone following the ideas, tips, suggestions, techniques, or strategies will become successful. The author and publisher shall have neither liability or responsibility to anyone with respect to any loss or damage caused, or alleged to be caused, directly or indirectly by the information contained in this book.

Touching Hearts ...
Changing Lives

"This book reflects who Jeff is and from personal experience, I can say that if you take the time to really feel the words that Jeff has written than they have the potential to incredibly impact your life. This isn't a book you should want to read, it's one you really have to read."

– B. Caswell, Student,
Harvard University, Harvard, MA

"Jeff breaks down the most complicated things about growing up. I highly recommend this book to you."

– E. Papp, Student,
University of Notre Dame, South Bend, IN

"*Pathways to Purpose* is an excellent roadmap to success. Every teen and even adult should read this book. It is a true illustration of how to be successful in all aspects of life! A true reminder of the way things were, yet forgotten, and how they should be now! A wonderful learning tool!"

– J. Hayes, Teacher/Union President,
Mascenic High School, New Ipswich, NH

"What makes Jeff unique is that he practices what he preaches. As a life long learner Jeff tells it straight, from the challenges of his youth to the success he has achieved today. Jeff has the uncommon ability to speak to teens on their level, sharing his wisdom in terms they can both relate to and remember. In a complicated world, Jeff's 'Keep it Simple' philosophy provides both direction **and** inspiration."

– Steve Spratt, Chairman of the Board,
Center for American Studies, School Board Member, NH

Dedication

To Tori and Taylor
I love you more than you'll ever know

And of course …

My wife, Marsha, whose unselfish support,
selfless attitude, and gentle spirit give me
the strength and courage to speak to the masses.
I love you!!

And lastly …

Mom and Dad for bringing me into this world
to educate, motivate, and serve education.

Special Thanks To:

It is rare that people ever accomplish anything without the help of others. I am very grateful to some very special people who have helped, guided, and truly supported me in the pursuit of my personal purpose in life. I would not be where I am today without their help.

My utmost sincere appreciation goes to my mom, dad, and my brother Rob. Thanks for bringing me into this world and for giving me the competitive spirit and motivation to be the best that I can be.

I truly appreciate my friend and mentor, Steve Spratt. Steve, you have always pulled through for me when I needed help, guidance, or educational advice. I value your friendship more than you'll ever know.

I am so blessed to have so many friends. I only wish that I could list each and every one of you but that would be a book of its own. Thank you to all of you. I love you and truly appreciate everything you give me.

Finally, I'd like to pay special thanks to my daughters, Tori and Taylor. I love you so much and anxiously await our time. To my nieces and nephews: Patrick, Meredith, Andrew, Heather, Ashley, Sydney and _____. You motivate me and I love you so much.

Table of Contents

A Message from Jeff Yalden ...

I love having the opportunity and privilege of speaking with teenagers. They keep it so real. They're never afraid to tell you what they think or what they're going to accomplish in their lives. The more teenagers I talk to the more I realize that although they dream of becoming successful, they have one major challenge to overcome: No one has ever taught them the essential principles for achieving success or how to define what success means to them as a person and as a member of society.

Society tells teenagers that if they go to school, they will become successful. While school plays a very important role in achieving success, there's more to it than that. A solid education is only one of the key elements in creating a successful life. Unfortunately, we often don't talk to teens about the other parts that are essential in not only creating professional success, but also personal success.

The other parts for creating success are included in what I call the REAL WORLD education. Skills such as goal setting, making connections, communicating with others, choosing a career, managing money, overcoming obstacles, and making the right choices are extremely important, not to mention the attitude, self-respect, role models, and the wisdom of others. All of these traits build upon the foundation provided by our schools. Teenagers need to learn these principles in order to create a successful future.

This book will provide teenagers with a road map for leading a successful life. More importantly, it teaches teenagers the essential principles for succeeding in the REAL WORLD.

Success does not begin when we graduate from college or land our first "big" job. Success has already started for you the moment you were conceived. Think about it: One sperm raced against five hundred million other sperm through a long tunnel for one egg. YOU WON! That means you are already successful. All you have to do now is capitalize on that success. Remember success begins to be more important to us as teenagers and continues to influence us for the rest of our lives. This is the time when we can put these key principles in motion and begin to create and shape our future.

This book is simple, to the point, and written in my language so you can easily understand these key elements of success. Although this book is not difficult to read, it can be life changing, so I caution you to proceed carefully. It contains some of the most valuable information teenagers will ever learn. Information that builds on the educational experience in every school whether public or private or large or small. This is information that should be taught in every school.

The principles in this book have one objective:

TO GIVE YOU THE READER A PATH FOR EXTREME PURPOSE IN YOUR LIFE! Then it's up to you to create the success you want.

CHAPTER 1

You Must
Think You Can

First things first. What do you believe about yourself? You must understand that the outcome of your life is a result of your actions and behaviors. Your actions and behaviors come as a result of what you personally believe. What do you believe?

What do you mean? Let's not start off too deep here. What do you first believe about yourself? I used to always believe that I wasn't capable; that I wasn't smart enough; that I didn't have the ability, the capability, or the intelligence to do something significant in my life.

What you believe is what creates your actions and behaviors. Your actions and behaviors are what will determine the outcome you are seeking in life.

Belief ☞ Behaviors ☞ Outcome

> *"The Outcome of your life is directly influenced by your behaviors, and your behaviors are influenced by what you believe."*
> *– Jeff Yalden*

I remember the early days of my life when I was told, "If you think you can make the shot, chances are you can make the shot. If you think you can pass the test, chances are you'll pass the test. If you think you can, you probably will, but if you think you can't, you probably won't." The lesson: If you think you can do something chances are good that you will, but if you think you can't, you probably won't.

We all dream of what we want or where we will be or whatever we will accomplish, and that is great. However, if you don't first believe in the dream, then the dream won't become true. You must first believe, because belief will give you the behaviors necessary to accomplish the dream.

I will never forget when I was in the Marine Corps stationed at Cecil Field, Naval Air Station in Jacksonville, FL. It was there when I truly realized the power of what you believe. If the belief is real and strong enough, then the outcome is more likely to be what you want.

I was going before the Meritorious Promotion Board to step up in rank. The four guys I was going up against all had at least one year's time in service ahead of me, but that didn't stop me from believing. They were more experienced, great guys, excellent Marines, well respected, and everyone thought I didn't have a chance because of the quality and experience of the competition I was going up against. But I believed in myself, and I knew my Marine Corps rules and regs better than anyone. I believed in my ability as a United States Marine. To me, it didn't matter what others thought or that the other Marines were more experienced. I believed in myself. I knew what I could do and what I could be!

Simply because I believed in myself, my behaviors changed. I did whatever it took to prepare myself for this one long day of interviews, tests, educational challenges, and whatever else was going to come my way. I was going to attack it because I was ready.

> "I visualized where I wanted to be, what kind of player I wanted to become. I knew exactly where I wanted to go, and I focused on getting there."
> – Michael Jordan

The day came and I could not have been more ready. "Bring it on," I thought. "Prepare to win and you'll win. Prepare to fail and you'll fail." I was prepared and knew that I won before the day took its course. I was so confident that I had won that I even put a new sticker on my car that had my new rank. I was probably a little too confident, but I just knew it. I didn't have to remove that sticker!

> "It all starts with a dream."
> – Jeff Yalden

Dreaming is a great thing to do. I love to daydream, but let me ask you something. If you dream of what you want but don't believe you are capable of achieving those dreams, then what does the dream mean? Dreams give you the mental picture of the success you want in life but believing causes you to take the actions necessary to make your dreams come true. Dreaming allows you to visualize the outcome; actions make that outcome become real. For me, dreaming always gave me the vision of the future I desired.

That day the dream was alive and running through my body like water flushed through a toilet. That was the dream, but the belief was stronger than the dream itself. The dream is where it all starts, but the belief gives you the behaviors to accomplish what some might think is impossible. All that matters is that you believe.

The problem with dreaming is that most people think their dreams will never come true.

I was one of those people once myself. But then one day I read in a book a quote that said, "You can do anything you put your mind to. If you can dream it, you can do it."

From that moment on, I never settled for anything less than my dreams. If I dreamed about achieving something, I pursued it until I had achieved it. Anything that I have ever accomplished in my life began with dreaming about it first.

Dreaming and believing that you will achieve your dream is half the battle. Once you are determined to achieve your dream nothing will stop you. Walt Disney once said, "All our dreams can come true – if we have the courage to pursue them."

That beautiful day ended with me winning unanimously and being selected as Corporal with only 19 months time in service. That was the fastest that anyone at Marine Corps Security Forces Atlantic had ever rose the ranks to Corporal. I became a Non-Commissioned Officer in the United States Marine Corps. Ooh-Rah!

I followed the same belief when it came time for the Marine-of-the-Year board. I believed, and that is all that mattered. I prepared because I knew I had a chance. I was confident. When you believe in yourself, you are willing to do whatever it takes to reach your goals. You will then prepare as much as you can.

To prepare, I went back to Parris Island, South Carolina where my former drill instructors were. I drove the six hours to meet with them. I made sure my uniform was squared away and ready to roll. I made sure my military bearing was in tip-top shape and that I didn't lose any discipline. They drilled me across the entire range of my Marine Corps knowledge and told me at the end of the day that I was ready. I was! Bring it on!

Well, I won Marine of the Year (two years in a row). How do you like that?

"If You Can Dream It, You Can Do It!"

Please take the time to remember this simple phrase. Dreams are not difficult to fulfill. We only think they are difficult because most people are afraid to pursue their dreams. Be different. You have the ability to achieve anything you desire. Simply make the decision to turn your dream into a goal. Then pursue your goal until you achieve it.

Remember the most important point: You can't turn your dream into a goal if you don't first believe you can accomplish the dream. If you believe in yourself and change your behaviors/attitudes as a result of what you believe you will accomplish what so many people, because of their fears, have never even tried to do.

Your success in life starts with the dream. To accomplish anything in life, you first must picture it in your mind, feel it in your heart, and desire it in your soul. Things are not achieved by chance. I will not disagree with luck playing a role at times, but to set out and accomplish something, you first must form a mental picture of how you would feel and what positive things will happen when you realize your dream.

All successful people dream, even some of the most popular people in the world. Their popularity didn't just happen. It came about because they believed in their ability to succeed and created the right mental image of their success.

No one has ever achieved anything great without first dreaming about it. Dreams form the mental picture of what we desire most in our life. The problem with dreaming is that most young people believe that their dreams can never be real. Or, they listen to those who tell them that they'll never achieve their dreams.

As you begin trying to accomplish certain goals in your life, you will meet people who will criticize you and try to bring you down. Stay away from these negative people. You don't need negative thinking people in your life.

Don't worry about what others think. It only matters what you think and believe. Don't try to please all the people in your life, as that is the quickest way to fail and be miserable. To be the best you can be you only have to please yourself.

If your friends do not support and encourage you, then they are not your true friends. True friends will believe in you and will help you figure out how to achieve your dreams.

Those who tell you that it can't be done are the very people who are afraid to pursue their own dreams. They are jealous of anyone who succeeds, because if you are moving forward and achieving goals in your life, then people will notice you and not notice them.

> *"Those who say it cannot be done*
> *should not interrupt those doing it."*
> *– Unknown*

Have a Positive Attitude

> *"A bad attitude is like pee in your pants.*
> *Everybody can see it, but only you can feel it."*
> *– Jeff Yalden*

Your attitude is critical in determining whether you succeed or fail. Your attitude is the foundation of the ideas you form in your mind. Your mind is like a computer. It stores anything you focus on. What you focus on is what you become and achieve. So don't make negative statements or think negative thoughts, because your brain will store them in your memory (just like a computer) and never forget them.

If you continuously store negative thoughts in your brain, you will eventually become a negative, non-achieving person. It may not be today, tomorrow, or next week. But be assured that one day it will happen to you.

Begin right here, right now, to make only positive statements and to think only positive thoughts. To get the results you desire in life you must change your thoughts. What you focus on, you will achieve, because thoughts are transformed into actions and actions produce results. If you change the way you think, then you can change the person you become. Anything that happens in life first begins as a thought.

Take your attitude to a new level and you will take your success to a whole new level as well. Develop a strong mental attitude and your chances of reaching your full potential are greater. Most people think negative thoughts rather than positive thoughts. It's simple – think positive thoughts if you want positive results.

Positive Attitude = Positive Results

Negative Attitude = Negative Results

Start right now to develop a positive attitude and begin focusing your thoughts on believing in yourself and your abilities. Before you realize it, you will be accomplishing whatever you believe.

The problem with most teenagers today is that they are more focused on instant gratification. They want it right now without having to work hard for it. "Now, not later," is their motto. Instead of having to work hard and earn what you desire, our nation has come to expect instant gratification.

Remember, the harder you work towards something, the better your attitude.

CHAPTER 2

Your Attitude
Is Everything

Attitude is everything. I know you have heard that before. Well, believe it. Nothing can be as influential as your attitude. Your attitude controls the choices you make. You make poor choices when you have a negative attitude. You make good choices by having a positive attitude. Keep it simple. You have to take charge and control your attitude every day. Nobody else can control your attitude. It's up to you. The best way to control your attitude is to understand the three main reasons why we even have a poor attitude in the first place.

Create the Self-Respect You Deserve

Many of us don't like ourselves and are constantly comparing ourselves to the people around us. We are looking for our identity and the meaning of life from others. Unfortunately, we are looking in the wrong places. To create a positive self-image we need to be happy with ourselves. This can only come as a result of our commitment to personal excellence.

It's easier said then done – I know. But when you have the right self-image, your life will blossom and you will feel capable of growing and succeeding. If you can't respect yourself, then you can't respect others. If you can't respect others, then others will not respect you. If you're not respected, then, of course, you'll be negative!

Self-image takes discipline, courage, and commitment. Having commitments in life is the best way to create oneself and a Purpose. Having a purpose in life is a key component in creating a positive self-image. Having commitments gives purpose to your very existence.

> *"The self is not, in essence, waiting to be discovered. The self is, in essence, waiting to be created."*
> – Dr. Anthony Campolo

Know That You Are SPECIAL

Think of it this way: At one time, you were a sperm. Yes, you were once a sperm. But you were not just any sperm. You were one of some 500,000,000 sperm. There was only one egg. 500,000,000 sperm and one egg! All you sperm once lined up at the starting line. You raced each other down a long tunnel. In the end, YOU WON! Isn't that amazing? One egg, and you were the one of the 500,000,000 sperm who won. The Olympics has nothing on you. You won the most important race ever!!! You are special.

Self-Esteem

Have you ever seen a relationship where a man treats the woman poorly? Do you know why this is? When the man doesn't think much of himself and doesn't believe in himself he builds himself up by tearing down his spouse. They do this to show that they are better by comparison. They build themselves up while tearing others down.

This is what I once did, and I am ashamed it. Needless to say, my relationship with the woman I treated poorly ended in a divorce.

At the time, I thought it was her fault, not mine. I didn't take personal responsibility for the situation at all. So I met another woman a short time later, and the same thing happened. I chose to build myself up by tearing her down. I wanted to show that I was better by comparison. Well, this relationship ended too, and I was to blame, although I still didn't take personal responsibility for my actions.

One day, though, I woke up and looked at myself in the mirror. I thought I was a loser. I decided to really look at myself and who I was. I didn't like who I saw, didn't like who I was, and didn't like what I was seeing down the road. I knew I had to make some changes. The first thing I did was start to change my self-esteem and take personal responsibility for my life.

Ladies, if you ever encounter a relationship like this, please get out and know that no man should ever treat you this way. Your personal self-respect has to be greater than any person, place, or thing, and you must know that this is not a healthy relationship. Love the skin you're in and accept nothing better than what you expect and deserve in a relationship.

Gentleman, you as well must like yourself. You *need* to like yourself. Look in the mirror. Do you like who you see? Who are you? Where you going? Are you taking personal responsibility for your self-esteem?

Failure Teaches Success

You will probably be like everyone and fail at something some time in your life. You will be in pursuit of accomplishing a dream when something holds you back. Your turn becomes an obstacle, a challenge, a course you did not want to pursue. You must understand that sometimes we do fail. Anyone who has become truly successful will tell you that their success didn't come easy. If success were easy then everyone would be successful beyond his or her wildest imagination and I wouldn't be writing to you now. The important thing is that you never quit or give up when you fail.

Successful people are not afraid to fail. Failure is a good teacher. Learn what you did wrong or what you have to do better to succeed next time. Failure is a part of trying. I would rather fail trying to accomplish something than never try at all. Don't quit when faced with failure; you may be closer to succeeding that you think.

Set your expectations higher than your friends and work hard towards them. Even if you fail or come up just short you will have learned valuable lessons that will serve you well for the rest of your life. You will also have accomplished more than the friends who didn't have any expectations or never tried to reach any dreams at all.

Thomas Edison failed about 2,000 times before finally inventing the light bulb. He didn't get discouraged. He didn't quit. He believed, which led to his behaviors. When he had an unsuccessful attempt, he would simply say that he was one step closer to finding the correct procedure.

Abraham Lincoln lost about eight elections before becoming President of the United States of America. Although he continued to lose elections, he never quit in pursuing his dreams.

Great accomplishments rarely occur on the first try. You will fail at some point. It's a part of life. Accept it, learn from it and get over it. Let it go. The way to overcome failure is to, first, realize that it happens, and then benefit from it. Failure will teach you valuable lessons about succeeding.

Find Role Models and Emulate Them

The type of people you associate with reflects the type of person you will become. If you associate with negative people, then you will eventually become a negative person. If you hang around positive people who have dreams and goals, then you will develop successful, winning characteristics. Find like-minded people such as yourself and surround yourself with them.

Study success. Find people who have had the kind of happiness and success that you would like to have in your life and then copy them. Learn what they are doing or what they have done, and they follow their path. *Success Leaves Clues!*

When you finish reading this book, take five minutes to think about those qualities you admire in other people. Which of those qualities would you like to have? Write down these ideas, memorize them, and begin practicing them every day. Soon, those qualities will become a habit and they will become the qualities you use to describe yourself!

Seek the Wisdom of Others

I have learned in my life that birds teach birds how to fly, and fish teach fish how to swim. I have also learned that women need to teach young ladies what it means to become a woman. The same is true for the men in this world. Men need to teach young men what it means to become a man.

The problem is that in today's society we are so caught up in our own lives. The busy schedules, the lost time, and the frequent interruptions prevent us from reaching all of our youth. This being said, you need to take the time to seek out influences in life that you trust and respect, whose opinions you value. Seek out their guidance, wisdom, and experience and don't ever be afraid to emulate them or ask them questions. You'll find out that they will be excited that you value them enough to seek their advice.

Two Types of People in the World

You and I are one of two types of people in this world. No more, no less, but we are one of these two groups. Are you In-Purpose or are you Out-of-Purpose? Everyone in our society fits into one of these two groups. Which one are you?

If You Are In-Purpose...

You're unselfish. You recognize it is not about you, but it is about everyone. You have love in your heart and want to reach out and help other people without expecting anything in return.

If You Are Out-of-Purpose...

You are completely selfish. You think everything in life revolves around you. You want instant gratification; you want things right now and don't want to have to wait!

It is my hope that if you are reading this book that you are In-Purpose. Or, you are reading this book to become In-Purpose. Either way, I congratulate you; you are on the right track. You will succeed and win when you are In-Purpose and separate yourself from those in your life who may be Out-of-Purpose.

Eight Most Powerful Phrases That Build Instant Respect

In today's society we have lost a lot of common respect for one another. Basic common courtesy has been put on the back burner or left out in the wind and blown away. If I can teach you nothing else but this, then this book was well worth writing. Here are the most powerful phrases that will take you places and earn you instant respect:

..Please	..Yes, sir
..Thank you	..No, sir
..Excuse me	..Yes, ma'am
..You're welcome	..No, ma'am

These are simple phrases that show you are a person of character and class. If you were taught these phrases as a child, I compliment your parents and/or guardians. If you were not taught these phrases, then THIS IS NO EXCUSE. Why can't you start using them today? Do not blame your lack of etiquette on others. It may be hard at first, but through everyday use they become a part of you and will eventually come naturally. By using these phrases, people will look up to you and respect you for your maturity.

Another pet peeve of mine is the type of handshake in use today. Nowadays, I feel like I am shaking a dead fish when I meet someone for the first time. What is up with this? Where does this come from? Is a firm handshake being taught? Obviously not! Well let me tell you the right way to shake someone's hand.

First, you step into the handshake because it shows self-confidence and that you are not intimidated by the other person. Second, you give a firm handshake; don't crush the bones in the other person's hand, but grasp the hand firmly. Then, look the person in the eye, as this builds trust and immediate respect. Be aware of how people shake your hand next time you greet someone. I bet you will see my point.

Another common courtesy I no longer see is holding the door for the next person. It used to be proper for a gentleman to hold the door for a lady. With the advent of equal rights it should be common for any person opening a door to hold it for the next person. So why isn't this true? It goes back to being In-Purpose or Out-of-Purpose. People who don't hold the door for the next person are Out-of-Purpose and only thinking about themselves. Next time you walk through a door, take a quick look behind you and hold the door with a smile. You will notice that being unselfish goes a long way; being In-Purpose gives you class and respect.

The use of common courtesy phrases, a firm handshake, and holding the door for others are easy, but often forgotten. Stop for a second and think about others, and use common courtesy in your everyday life. You will feel the change and reap the benefits.

Avoid Negative Influences

We are surrounded by negative influences everywhere we go. For example, we are influenced by the media all around us. Newspapers and televisions provide us with news and entertainment that enriches our daily lives. On the other hand, these same sources are filled with an abundance of gratuitous sex and violence. We as a society are surrounded by negative influences no matter where we turn. What can be done about this? There is a simple solution. The media and the entertainment industry are a part of our daily existence and will continue to be forever. How it influences us is our choice. We know what is positive and what is negative. Therefore, if we know that something is negative and doesn't benefit us, then we should turn ourselves away by not purchasing, watching, or partaking in a negative act or event.

Another negative influence in our lives is when we choose the easy wrong over the hard right. Every day we are faced with choices that can, and will, determine the quality of our lives. This is why making positive choices are so important to our future success. Let me ask you this question, "Do you know the difference between right and wrong?" Every student I ask knows the difference, so I will assume that you know the difference as well. Therefore, when presented with a situation with right or wrong consequences, we should all be able to make the right choice. My point is that since we know the difference, then we should be expected to do the right thing regardless of whatever negative influences surround us.

Another negative influence is the lack of responsibility we are expected to take for our actions. Too many times in society I hear that we are trying to baby our youth in order to take the pressure of responsibility off of them. While this may seem like kindness, it is truly a disservice. Children who learn that they are not accountable for their actions tend to expect this treatment throughout their lives. When you make the wrong choice you have to hold yourself accountable for it. You have to accept the consequences of your decision. How does one grow up and become a mature member of society if he or she has not learned to accept responsibility? We need to be expected to make good choices and accept the consequences of our actions no matter what our age.

Remember: Avoid negative outside influences, make good choices, and take responsibility for your actions!

You will encounter a time in your life when you are going to have to choose to upgrade the quality of influences in your life. Are you better off as a result of the people you hang out with or are you worse off as a result of them? You have to take personal responsibility as to who your influences are. Who you associate with is who you become, and who you become is a result of the people you associate with.

It takes courage to separate yourself from friends. However, you are the only one who knows if others bring you down or make you better. Here's a tip. Pay attention to what you are doing when you are out with your friends. Is it really what you feel you want to do? If it isn't, you're hanging out with the wrong people. Make the right choice, and do it now rather than later. You'll save yourself a lot of time in the future and many headaches.

CHAPTER 3

Never Lose Sight
of the Fundamentals

Very often in music, theatre productions, and sporting events you'll see that the successful performers have mastered the fundamentals in their chosen field. Fundamentals are the basic ingredients for success. How can a musician be great if she doesn't know how to play a C sharp? How can a basketball player be a star if he can't make a free throw or a lay-up? Every professional was once a beginner. They had to learn the fundamentals before they were able to progress. But at no point are they ever able to forget the building blocks that we call the fundamentals.

> *"The first problem for all of us, men and women, is not to learn but to unlearn."*
>
> *– Gloria Steinem*

This quote is a favorite of mine. It takes me back to Parris Island when I was in boot camp. The purpose of boot camp is to break down the recruit's previous habits and build them back up with the fundamentals developed by the United States Marine Corps standards.

We are creatures of habit, some good and some bad. This is exactly why boot camp lasts 12-13 weeks; it takes time to break the habits that have been a part of our lives for so long. It is when we can abandon our habits and form new ones that we learn to "unlearn" and develop anew.

Having said that, we need to look at life as a game and master the fundamentals in the game of life. We master the game of life by being fundamentally sound. Simple! Being a person of character, class, and unselfishness are the fundamentals of life and the basics of success and significance.

Be a Person of Character

Character is who you are in the dark; it's what you would do if you knew that you would never be found out. Think about it. How would you react to a situation if you knew you would never be found out? How you answer is a true test of your character. As simple as it sounds, in the long run, being a person of character helps you maintain a good attitude. You don't have to put on a mask, nor do you have to constantly be on the lookout. Why? You aren't living a lie. Being a person of character gives you the freedom to enjoy life without hiding anything. A person of character always wins in the long run.

> *"Be more concerned with your character than your reputation, because your character is who you are, while your reputation is merely what other people think you are."*
> *– John Wooden*

My brother is someone whom I really admire. He is a top Special Agent with the United States Secret Service. I call him Robocop. He travels aboard Air Force One with the President. It's a big job with lots of stress and great stories to tell. Being a Secret Service Agent requires a person to be of good moral character.

Before becoming a Secret Service Agent, my brother spent some time at the Naval Academy's Preparatory School in Bristol, Rhode Island. It was there that he learned about character. He passed his military experiences onto me, his younger brother. I think he thought it would be funny to treat me the way he was treated at the academy. I didn't think having him home was fun at all.

When my brother was home; it was my duty to wake him at 0645. Since he was about 6'7" and weighed close to 270, there was not much I could do to refuse his request. By 0700, I had to have his breakfast prepared and ready for him. At 0710, I had to clear the table and immediately report to the front foyer of our house where I had to "push the ground" to the tune of about 100 push-ups at his command. He thought it was funny that he didn't get tired when I pushed. Then, at about 0740, I would have to rebound 100 free throws for him. Yeah, this was great! And all this before the bus would come to take me to school.

Often times, my brother would serve as my babysitter. On these occasions he had more time to discipline me. One night, my parents went out and left us alone. As my parents drove out of the driveway, my brother threw me in the closet. A few days later (it was only a few minutes but seemed like a few days), my brother returned and he asked me, "Jeff, what do you see in there?" I was in tears and didn't think he was very funny. I replied, "Rob, this isn't funny, let me out. It's dark. I don't see anything. I do feel a lot of coats around here though." He said, "Jeff, I am going to teach you one of the most important lessons you will ever learn." He paused, and then said, "Jeff, what you see is your character." I was mad at him for locking me in the closet, but I can honestly say he made me understand what character is really all about.

I am thankful today for what my brother taught me. A lot of my successes today are a result of listening to Robocop. Perhaps this is one of the reasons I say we should always listen to those older than us because they might have something valuable to teach us. I speak about character during my programs, but sometimes the best examples are illustrated by the words of others around me. A few years ago, I met a great gentleman in Jefferson, Ohio when I was speaking at the Jefferson schools. His name was Don Lee, and when we were talking about character, he said:

> *"Your character is the only thing that walks back from the grave."*
> *– Don Lee, Ashtabula, Ohio*

How true! People will never remember the car you drove, the house you lived in, or the size of your bank account. What they will remember and reflect upon will be how you lived your life and what kind of person you were.

Most things in life are material but your character is the foundation of your life and will outlast them all. Know your character and be yourself; be who you are in the dark.

People are comfortable with people who have class because the people who have class are comfortable with themselves. People of class don't run scared, they don't make

If you want to build Character:	If you want to tear down Character:
Help others	Call people names
Stay on task	Break rules
Tell the truth	Be irresponsible
Show respect	Hurt others
Be fair	Be selfish
Be honest	Get even
Follow rules	Be lazy
Be responsible	Give up
Show kindness	Tell lies
Do the right thing	Don't try your best
Have a good work ethic	Steal

excuses, and they don't hide. Most importantly, people of class don't build themselves up by tearing others down. People of class have respect for all and fear of none.

Like character, class is important to maintain the right attitude and fundamentals. A person of class is empathetic and compassionate to others. Because of this, a person of class makes a great leader because he or she can instantly be trusted and respected.

> *"Criticism is the autobiography on oneself."*
> *– James Russell Lowell*

One example of a class act is Coach Mike Kryziewski, the head coach of Duke University basketball. He is a man who exemplifies class, character, and what all leaders should be like. He is one of the most respected people in all of college basketball because of who he is as a person, as demonstrated in the following story.

It was March 29, 1999 and the NCAA Division I National Championship of college basketball had just ended. Duke University had just lost to the University of Connecticut. This was an upset in college basketball since Duke was favored to win. After the game they interviewed Coach Kryziewski. You would expect that a coach of a losing team would be discouraged, furious, and very upset. But, in typical Coach Kryziewski fashion, he stood there in front of cameras, newspaper reporters, and the entire world of sports with a smile on his face. When asked how he felt to lose to Connecticut, he stood there with grace, poise, and a smile on his face and said something I will never forget: "I can't be sad. I can't. I don't coach for winning games; I coach for relationships."

Wow! This is one of the greatest coaches of the game. For him to say it's not about wins and losses but about relationships exemplifies good character. This man said it all. It is about the relationships. Now that is class. Unselfishness is when a person thinks about others before thinking about themselves.

Life is not about you; life is about everyone. People have more respect for you when they know that you are a person who truly cares about others. My life became more significant when I stopped thinking so much about myself and started thinking about other people. For me this was hard since I had always been selfish. When I started to see the benefits of being unselfish, I became more successful, more income started to come my way, my quality of life changed, and, most important, my overall happiness increased.

When people become depressed or bored, it is because they are being selfish and only thinking about themselves. Please understand I am not talking about clinical depression, as I know this is an illness. What I am saying is that people tend to get depressed or bored simply because they are thinking about themselves too much and not others. Look around you and get over yourself already!

CHAPTER 4

Have
Commitments in Life

The following three simple rules by which I live have become my commitments in life:

Rule #1 – Do What Is Right

Rule #2 – Do the Best You Can

Rule #3 – Treat Others the Way You Would Want
Them to Treat You

That is it. I try not to complicate things, so everything I do lies within these parameters I have set as commitments for myself. Our commitments in life create our identity. I would like to outline these three rules, as they have become the cornerstones of my success.

Take Personal Responsibility

I wrecked my dad's car when I was a junior in high school. He made me pay for the damages. Two weeks later I wrecked his other car, and he made me pay for those damages as well. I started my life about $20,000 in debt. However, I learned a great lesson as a result of this.

One night my mother shared this with me and I will never forget her words. My mother said to me, "Son, when you

are ready and willing to accept responsibility for the circumstances, conditions, behaviors, and most importantly for
the choices of your life, it will be then and only then that you
will have the power to change your future."

Wow! Those are words I will never forget.

I grew up and didn't take responsibility for my life. I didn't
care to. I didn't take responsibility for my attitude, my grades,
and my life. I just didn't.

Well, that came back to hurt me and made me who I
am today. I am grateful for what happened because it is
who I am, and without this happening I don't think I would
be half the man I am today.

At 18 years old, I graduated from high school without
plans for anything else. I didn't choose to go to one of the
three colleges that accepted me. I was in a relationship and
she was my everything.

I chose to join the Marine Corps and that was a blessing
in my life. I continued dating this one woman who later became my wife and the mother of my two daughters, whom
I dedicate this book to.

I learned that no matter what happens in life we have to
first take the responsibility for all circumstances, conditions,
actions, etc. Only when we take responsibility can we make
a change and take action.

Years ago, while going through some challenges and
being hospitalized for depression, my grandmother asked
me to listen to a tape. It was this tape by Lou Holtz (at the
time he was the head football coach of the University of

Notre Dame) that changed my life. My career today is also a result of this very same tape and the influence of Lou Holtz.

Rule #1 – Do What Is Right

We know the difference between right and wrong; therefore, we should do what's right and avoid what's wrong. When you do something wrong, you need to understand and accept the fact that you are accountable for your actions and be willing and ready to be held responsible. You can avoid this by simply doing the difficult right over the easy wrong.

You will encounter times in your life when you have to go against what makes you happy in order to do the right thing. This is called RIGHTEOUSNESS OVER HAPPINESS. Sometimes being mature helps you to make good choices in your life.

The FOUR T's

When making choices in life, you need to remember The Four T's and how they benefit you. The Four T's stand for: Take Time to Think.

Did you know that 80% of Fortune 500 CEOs wake up an hour early every day to take time to think about their day? They prepare for their meetings, what's ahead for them, what circumstances they will encounter, people they need to talk to or see, etc. What do you do? Do you take time for yourself every day to prepare and think about what you need to do?

Rule #2 – Do the Best YOU Can

The key word in this rule is YOU. It's about you, not someone else. Be selfish here and do your very best in whatever it may be.

Many people believe that the average person is basically lazy and wants everything handed to him or her. I agree. I have found in my own experience that most people don't want to have to work hard or extend themselves. This attitude concerns me, because we are in an era where too many people want things without having to work for them. If you are lazy and unwilling to have to work hard then what success can you achieve? No one will hand you success or happiness if you are unwilling to work for it yourself.

So, the question remains, "Do you want success and happiness?" Well then, be ready to work for it! One of the reasons why I am where I am today is because of my work ethic.

My motto is this: I must demand more of myself than anybody else demands of me! I want to be the BEST! Work hard, push yourself, demand greatness of yourself and your abilities, and accept nothing less than the very best from yourself. Only then will you reap the rewards of your work.

When you do the best YOU can, nobody can expect anything more of you. In the classroom, out of the classroom, on the athletic field, off the athletic field, in a part-time job, or in any activity that you are participating in, just do your very best and you will be a winner. I don't mean that you will always win the game, but I do mean that you will feel that you have won within yourself. Whether you win or lose is not important, but being proud of your accomplishments and how you played is fundamental to your commitment to excellence. If you are doing your best, then people will know you have a commitment to excellence.

Rule #3 – Treat Others the Way You Would Want Them to Treat You

Do unto others as you would have done to you. Basically, treat and respect others the same way you would want others to treat and respect you.

I live my life simply by this: I don't care if you are black, white, Jewish, Protestant, Catholic, Christian, Muslim, Hindu, male, female, straight, or gay. I don't care if you drive a BMW, a Honda Accord, or a John Deere Tractor. I feel that we are all one and nobody is any better than anybody else.

Wouldn't it be great if everyone lived by this rule? Then we would be without hate, prejudice, crime, and violence. We'd all get along much better. Life would be great.

The golden rule is so powerful and so meaningful. Why can't we be more helpful to others instead of hurtful? Why can't we all have more love in our hearts than hate in our souls? Where does true equality begin? It begins with us. We need to accept that people are born a certain way and make choices that are beyond our control.

For example, does a black baby, a white baby, a Jewish infant, or Catholic infant, perhaps even a person who is gay have any say or choice in how they were born? People don't choose the circumstances of their birth, but we can all make the choice to accept other people for who they are.

Make the right choice. I challenge you to make the first move to respect all people each and every day, one person at a time. And it starts here with you reading this. Now go out there and have a little more respect, a little more love, a little more understanding, and a little more compassion and empathy towards others.

I'd like to share with you a personal story that affected my life in many ways. Little did I know that my life would change as a result of what I experienced. I don't wish what I went through on anyone, but the experience has taught me much.

February 26, 1992 – Cecil Field
Naval Air Station, Jacksonville, FL

He was one of my Marines who chose to show up late back from a four day weekend that we call a "96" in the Marines. It means 96 hours away. His name was PFC Eisenburg, one of my Marines at Cecil Field Naval Air Station in Jacksonville, Florida from December 1990 to January of 1993. I remember PFC Eisenburg very well because he was always by himself and didn't really have too many friends. His uniform was never pressed out and his boots never really shined. He may not have been the best Marine, but he was one of our Marines.

The morning of February 25 of 1992, PFC Eisenburg showed up late for duty and missed formation. As a disciplinary punishment I put him on a 24- hour post. It was my responsibility to ensure that he was armed and on duty at all times. At 0400 on the morning of February 26, I got up to see how Eisenburg was doing. We talked for several hours as he shared with me a lot about his past and current life. He was down and depressed and shared with me that his fiancée of five years had just ended their relationship. Also, he told me his mother had left him when he was young, his father was in jail for drugs, and he hadn't seen his brother for about three years. Hours passed as we had a meaningful conversation.

At about 0730, he showed me a picture of himself, his fiancée, and his brother. After a few minutes of reflection, he dropped the picture at my feet and walked off in tears to his room down the hall. After a few minutes, I walked to his room. As I approached the room, I noticed that the door was slightly ajar. I pushed it open, and Eisenburg was sitting in his chair with a 9mm handgun at his chin, ready to take his own life. Careful of my every move I looked at him, maintaining my sharp military bearing, and said, "Eisenburg, don't do it." He looked at me and said, "Nobody cares about me." I replied, "I care," and he said, "Maybe you're the only one."

You see, he wasn't a very good Marine, but that didn't make him a bad person. People just didn't give him a chance. Some were too quick to make comments or certain gestures towards him and some just ignored him. This really affected him and nobody really knew how he felt. I was standing about four or five feet away from him, desperate to find something to say that would be meaningful. I wanted so bad to jump across the room and knock the gun out of his hands. But I tried to be patient and talk him out of pulling the trigger and taking his own life.

At exactly 0738, on February 26, 1992, as I looked Eisenburg in the eye and he looked at me, his last words were, "Maybe you're the only one." He pulled the trigger as I stood there in front of him. As people arrived to help, I knew he was already dead. Did I fail in saving him? My answer is, "No."

I wish he hadn't died, but I am secure in the fact that I did everything I could at the time. His decision was already made before I entered the room. At least I got to tell him I cared before he died. I still miss him.

Unselfishness

"One of the biggest questions people will always ask about you is – Do you care about me?"

– Jeff Yalden

One of the reasons I speak so heavily on the topic of unselfishness and caring is simply because of this story. I hope that because I shared with you this tragic day in my life that you will open up and care a little more about people.

We see lots of stories in the news lately about students wanting to kill other students or take their own lives because they feel they were picked on. This would stop if we could all do our part to stop hurting others and start helping instead. I hope that you can honestly say that you have never been the cause of someone else's pain. There is a great word in our vocabulary: HEART. In order to have HEART we need to show we care. Within the word HEART is another word: HEAR. We care through listening which also gives us the word EAR. There is a reason why we have two EARS and only one mouth; maybe we should use them in that ratio. We should listen two times more than we talk. Listening can make all the difference in the world when someone is in pain because then they know you care.

CHAPTER 5

Say No to Drugs

"I've never heard anyone stand before an audience and say, 'I am successful today because of drugs and alcohol.'"

– Jeff Yalden

Recently, I spent a day with the Drug Czar in Washington D.C. during the PRIDE World Drug Free Conference. We spoke about the use of alcohol and drugs amongst youth today. His comment was that we were at an all time low with the use of drugs and alcohol. I enjoyed hearing those comments, however, I was left to ask why is it so highly talked about in the media. After all, when we publicize something, it makes it more popular.

I personally don't think that drugs and/or alcohol is THE problem. Is it a problem? It's an issue, but here is THE problem: Students feeling the need to be accepted.

Today's youth have so many more opportunities than we had twenty years ago. Think about it. With technology today, youth have more access to gain knowledge and find information; they also have more pressure to perform.

Trying to keep up in a constantly demanding world, our youth feel the need to be accepted by others and do what others are doing so that they will easily be accepted by them. It's not the drugs, the alcohol or the smoking that's cool; it's the people doing these things that our teenagers think are cool. So to fit in they join in. When a person's self esteem is not where it should be, then the person feels the need to be accepted and he or she will do anything that is perceived as "cool."

Therefore, having said that, you need not feel the need to be accepted rather you need to first learn to accept yourself and not be so caught up in what others think.

Make the Right Choices

Every minute of every day you make a decision. You are constantly making choices. You choose what time to get up, what time to go to bed, what to wear, what to eat, who to talk to, who not to talk to, to do your homework or not to do your homework. You choose whether you are going to be on time or you are going to be late. You choose whether you are going to commit to giving your best effort.

Decisions are so powerful. Each and every decision you make every day will shape and define your future. Making one wrong choice can change your life forever. The problem with making decisions is most people think, "It will never happen to me!" It can happen to you, whatever "it" may be.

Labor Day weekend 2003 was an awesome weekend just like any other Labor Day I have lived before. This one was slightly different though.

One of my former student leaders at a local high school where I live was a great girl with a great future. I will say her name is "Suzy." Some people say that what happened wasn't her fault, but that a simple choice could have prevented her death.

It was late Friday night about 1:00 a.m. when "Suzy" was with her boyfriend "Sam" and two other students at a local Dunkin Donuts. They were drinking and having a good time. "Suzy" wasn't drinking alcohol, and there was no alcohol in the car. However, the other kids were drinking that night.

As the night wore on, "Suzy" and "Sam" were racing home along a major route where the speed limit is 45 mph. It's a winding road that travels alongside the river up into the mountains. "Sam" was driving about 80-90 mph in a 45 mph zone. The choice here is that "Suzy" could have chosen not to get into the car, knowing that "Sam" had been drinking. However, she chose to go home and chose to buckle up.

The attitude that "it will never happen to me, we'll be fine, everything will be cool, we'll make it home no problem" got the best of all of them. "Sam" lost control of his Honda Accord while going around a bend. The car hit the guardrail, hit the rock wall, spun a few times, and flipped over a couple of times. They were all alive and okay. Thankfully they were wearing their seat belts. The second choice here is that "Suzy" could have told him to slow down. Perhaps she did, but he didn't. I don't know.

What I do know is that there was another car that night at Dunkin Donuts. A 24-year-old guy who had just purchased a brand new Ford Mustang was with a few other students from another high school.

They too were racing that night on the way home. They too were doing about 80-90 mph; however, they didn't see the car in the middle of the road. As they came around the corner where "Suzy" and "Sam's" car was flipped over in the middle of the road, they hit it.

The end result is that Labor Day weekend when people were supposed to be enjoying one of the final weekends on the boat, having fun, and enjoying the weather, the people of this local school were gathered at the high school mourning the loss of a great student whom they will never forget.

You see, that car coming up the road didn't see the flipped car, and it collided right into the passenger's side door where "Suzy" was sitting with her seat belt on.

Raise your self-esteem, love yourself, and believe in yourself. Be selfish here for a second. You don't need to be accepted by others. You have to accept yourself. When you do that, others will feel the need to be accepted by you.

You know that drugs and alcohol are not good for you and are illegal. I will never say DON"T do drugs or drink. You have heard that a thousand times before. Instead, make good choices and know that no drug or drink will ever make you happy with yourself or with your career. Drugs and alcohol will never help you get ahead. They will only hurt you.

The choice is yours, but here is some help to understand further: What do you think you possibly gain from using drugs? They cause people to self-destruct, families to be ruined and broken-up, and careers destroyed. As a time bomb will explode, so will your mind, body, and your life if you choose to be friends with drugs.

According to The U.S. Department of Education, a 16-year-old girl told doctors that her entire life was focused on crack. The amazing thing about this is that she was interviewed on a Friday and had used crack for the first time the previous Monday. Within five days the drug had completely taken over her life.

You can't tell me that drugs are cool and that everyone is doing it. Everyone is not doing it. How cool do you think it would be if drugs got you kicked out of school? Then you'll have difficulty getting into college. You say, "I'm not going to college." Therefore, you think it won't matter. Well, the military won't take you either. Once you get that negative mark on your "Life Report Card" for messing with drugs, you can't erase it. But you can turn your life around. If you're messing with drugs, simply MAKE THE RIGHT CHOICE TODAY and stop.

If you make a mistake in life and choose to turn your life around, please write me to tell me about it. I'll be happy for you. Nobody is perfect, but it takes heart, courage, character, and class to turn your life around. That to me is a successful person who wants to succeed.

Do you think you will be cool if you mess with drugs and jump out of a window because you think you can fly? It happens.

Drugs can cause you to do things that you normally wouldn't do. They may cause you to hurt or even kill someone. They can even kill you. Do you want to take the chance of dying just to get a cheap high?

Think Before You Do Drugs

> "You might do drugs but it is the Drugs that DO you."
> – Jeff Yalden

Don't use drugs to get high. Use life to get high. Get the natural high from friends, family, hobbies, sports, theatre, music, etc. Get high from doing your best and seeing the results in school. It is the positive things in life that can give you so much more of a high than any drug ever can give you. Drugs don't help you to enjoy your life; you help you enjoy your life.

Nobody can help you stay away from drugs. No mom, dad, brother, sister, girlfriend, boyfriend, or relative, teacher, coach can make the choice for you. Only you can make the choice. The choice is yours.

I can write everything in this book, but still only you can make the choice. I personally have never in my life ever picked up a cigarette. I didn't drink in high school, didn't drink in the Marine Corps, and don't drink now. I just never have. It never appealed to me, and I never felt the pressure to drink when at the parties. I just didn't and that is it.

Drugs take the lives and careers of some of the greatest people. For example, just look at the life of Len Bias, a great athlete coming out of the University of Maryland. He was drafted by the Boston Celtics and signed a multi-million dollar contract. He was expected to become one of the greatest players of all time.

The very night he was drafted he made a choice that killed him. He never earned a penny of his contract. Drugs killed him. What a sad story.

How about Rush Limbaugh with painkillers? They got the best of him and now he is dealing with the embarrassment of checking into rehab. I am proud of him that he is handling the situation correctly. I am glad that he sought help before it was too late.

How about Chris Farley? Man, he was one of the best actors in the world. Remember on *Saturday Night Live* how he did that skit about Matt Foley the motivational speaker? I love that and loved him. It is sad to see that with all that talent he was still not satisfied with himself. He sought the artificial high because personally he was missing something within himself. He needed the women, the fame, the money, the alcohol, and the drugs. Now he is dead.

Alcohol Is a Drug

Many of our youth today don't think that alcohol is a drug. It is. It impairs your thinking, your reflexes, and your ability to make rational choices. Alcohol abuse can lead to medical problems, unplanned pregnancies, suicide attempts, crimes such as assault and rape, and AIDS. Consider the following facts that were recently reported by SADD (Students against Destructive Decisions):

- One in three college students now drink primarily to get drunk.

- 95% of violent crimes on campus are alcohol related.

- 90% of all reported campus rapes occur when alcohol is being used by either the assailant or the victim or both.

- 60% of college woman who have acquired STD's, sexually transmitted diseases, including AIDS and genital herpes, were under the influence of alcohol at the time they had intercourse.

Perhaps these stats don't do anything for you. Well then here are some that might make you think again.

- A 19-year-old Lewis University student fatally shot himself with a .38 caliber revolver in a game of Russian roulette. According to his roommate, the student apparently spun the chamber and pulled the trigger several times before the round fired, killing him instantly. Both students had been drinking prior to the incident.

- An 18-year-old University of Colorado freshman was killed after being thrown from the roof of a vehicle. The 18-year-old driver who had been drinking, as had all four passengers, tried to take a curve too fast and went off the side of the road, rolling the vehicle on its top.

- A Southwest Missouri State University freshman died after jumping off a seventh-story building balcony during spring break on South Padre Island. Police said the student was tampering with a fire hose when security caught him. The student ran down the corridor and threw himself over the balcony. An autopsy showed that the 18-year-old student had been drinking.

You are a smart person. You made the choice to read this book. I didn't want to spend a lot of time talking about this, but I thought it was necessary. Hey, just make the right choice. If you need further help, please visit my website, as I have a whole section on who to call for the help you need.

It is when we take the time to think about our choices before we act upon them that our inner-self will direct us to RIGHTEOUSNESS. Sometimes this is hard because it will require patience and going against what makes us happy. However, it is the Four Ts that will always help us do the right thing.

Remember: Do the difficult right over the easy wrong.

CHAPTER 6

Write Down Your Goals

Goals are very important, but they have a beginning and an end. You reach your goals. You set them, go after them, and do everything in your power to attain them in the time you set for yourself. The difference is that your purpose in life is never ending. You don't strive to reach your purpose; it simply keeps you on track towards the goals you have set for yourself.

The purpose of goals is to focus your attention. You will not be able to stay focused or measure your progress unless you clearly define your goals. When you have a clear understanding of your goals and can visualize what you want, then you will have the desire to work hard to reach it. The desire will ignite the spark inside you that pushes you towards the success. Once you feel the desire, your determination to succeed becomes more powerful than any feeling of giving up.

Not having a goal is like trying to drive a car without a road map to a place you have never visited. How can you expect to reach your destination without proper direction? The same is true of anything you wish to accomplish in life. You need a plan – a road map that leads you from point A to B.

So here is the time for you to write down some of your goals. The following SMART formula will help you. Write on a piece of paper the following:

Goals I Want to Accomplish

List the goals you WILL accomplish daily, weekly, monthly, and annually. Have goals for one year, three years, five years and even beyond. Write down any and all of your dreams. Some you will reach, some you will not and some will change. The important thing is to write them down.

Do this every year, reviewing last year's goals and adding new ones. Rewrite your goals. See them, read them, know them, list them, and change them whenever you want. The important thing is to write them down.

Write down as many as you desire. Don't be shy. This is your chance to dream big. Write down places you would like to visit, people you would like to meet, activities you would like to do, and things you would like to achieve. Write down whatever you desire in your heart.

After making your list, write beside each goal the exact date you WILL accomplish your goal. This is an important part of goal setting because it places a deadline on your goal. You have now obligated yourself to achieve it by a certain date because you are creating a contract with yourself. Take it another step further and tell someone about it asking them to help hold you to it making it even harder for you to give up.

The contract with yourself stores the goals in your mind, just as you would store data in a computer. Now your list of goals becomes your checklist. It's the same as if you had listed items on a grocery checklist. A grocery checklist allows you to see and remember what you need to get at the store. A goal checklist allows you to see and remember what you desire to achieve in life.

Once your mind is programmed with the data of what you WILL accomplish, you begin moving toward achieving your goals. Before you realize it, you start to achieve your goals. Your dreams start to become realities!

It's like magic when you write down your goals and place a deadline on achieving them. Somehow, you begin to achieve them.

At the end of your goal checklist, after you have written down ALL of your goals, it is very important for you to sign and date the paper. This commits you to pursuing them because it is now a formal contract with yourself. Now you have no one to blame but yourself if you fail to pursue your goals.

Look at your goals every day when you wake up and/or before you go to bed. Keep showing and telling your mind that these are the things you WILL accomplish in your life.

SMART Goals

SMART stands for: Specific, Measurable, Attainable, Realistic, and Timely.

Specific –

Be specific as to exactly what you want. You can't be too specific. Write it all down. Go for it.

Do you want a car? What kind of car? What color? Two doors or four doors? Hatchback, wagon, sedan, SUV, sports car or convertible?

Do you want a house? Ranch, split level, four bedrooms, three bedrooms, two baths or three baths? Two-car garage or three-car garage? Heated garage? Do you want an office, play room, furnished basement for the big screen television so you can watch your sports or just go down for the surround sound and chill while watching a nice movie?

Measurable –

Lay your goals out as to when you want to attain them. How long will it take you? By when do you want to achieve the goal(s)? Have goals that are daily, weekly, monthly, and annually. Here is an example:

Daily –	**1 Year –**
Weekly –	**3 Years –**
Monthly –	**5 Years –**
3 Months –	**10 Years –**
6 Months –	

Attainable –

Can you do it in the time you have allotted yourself? Are you comfortable with the tasks you've outlined or are you trying to do too much too quickly? Have you set aside time just to chill? Is it really attainable?

Realistic –

Make your goals as realistic as you can. You can say, "Jeff when I grow up I want to play in the NBA." But if you are 27 years old, 5'2" in the 9th grade, one leg shorter than the other, and blind in one eye, then this goal probably is not realistic. Spend this time defining goals you desire and expect to achieve. Setting realistic goals doesn't mean thinking small. It's not a convenient way of limiting your dreams. If you start writing your goals with a poor attitude it's easy to say any dream is unrealistic. Don't go there. It's a trap.

Timely –

Are you giving yourself enough time to reach the goals you are setting? Are you shortening the timeline too much? You probably can't graduate college in two years. I mean you can, but should you reevaluate the time you are giving yourself?

Your Purpose

Your purpose in life is now your goals. Your purpose is what you do every day to reach and achieve this great success you are after. By staying in purpose you turn your desires into actions every day.

Without a purpose you have nothing driving you to reach the goals. Your purpose is never-ending. It is the track that keeps the train on course. It is the breakfast that holds you over to your next meal. It is the thread that connects the day from morning to afternoon to night.

When your friends want to go to the party and drink, but you are thinking that you have something else more productive to do, something that you haven't completed yet, that's when you are thinking of your purpose.

Your purpose keeps you on track and gives you the motivation to accomplish the day's work when the going gets tough. Your purpose gives you direction to reach your goals in the shortest amount of time.

Jeff makes a strong point.

Notice the sweat as Jeff works the
program in San Salvador.

Jeff took his good friend Steve
to San Salvador.

Jeff facilitates a youth leadership
conference in San Salvador,
El Salvador, Central America.

Jeff's booth at a conference hoping
someone would buy a book.

Play like a champion today . . .
Jeff loves the University of Notre Dame.

Jeff speaks in Cincinnati, Ohio.

Jeff's audience is what motivates him
day in and day out.

Jeff shares a funny story
with his audience.

This is Chase. Jeff's best friend.

Jeff works a teacher in-service program
in West Virginia.

No, I do not have my back on my audience. They were just on two sides of the bleachers.

Jeff motivates his Marines in 1992.

CHAPTER 7

Plan for the Future – NOW

Most of your life will include the career you choose. Do you have any idea what you want to do when you're out of school? If not, you're not alone. I would bet that 90% of the teenagers in America have no clue. I would also bet that the majority of the 90% who don't have a clue don't even think about it. I never did.

You need to start getting a clue, NOW! You're not expected to know what will be your career for the rest of your life. But you do need to begin researching certain careers. Why? Your life will revolve around your career. You will most likely work five days and 40 hours a week, 235 days, and 2,040 hours a year, and about 7,000 days and 80,000 hours of your life. I bet you never thought of it like that. Now think of this doing something you hate. Not something to look forward to, is it?

How many times have you heard someone say, "I hate my job?" You don't want to be in a situation where you hate going to work every day.

Choosing a Career

Start by finding something meaningful, rewarding, and fulfilling. This will make you happy. If you identify the things that make you happy you will begin to get a clearer idea of what you may want to do when you get out of school. It may be acting or sports, mathematics or music, speaking or science. The key is to identify the activities which make you feel good about what you've accomplished.

Ask yourself the following two questions. They will help you to decide which career will make you happy:

1. Which career really excites and energizes me?
2. Which career would make me feel most fulfilled?

Once you have identified a career that you think makes you fulfilled, gives you meaning, and you think will be rewarding, then make a commitment to yourself to pursue your ambition. Gather as much information as you can. If you can find someone who works in that field talk to them and find out what they like or don't like about their job. Don't listen to those who try to discourage you. Many people dream of working a certain job or in a particular industry. But few accomplish their dreams because they listen when others tell then that it's not possible.

You have the ability to pursue and land any career you desire. Don't listen to those who try to discourage you. These are probably the very people who have never, and will never, have the career they desire for themselves. Just because they haven't done it, they think that you can't. They're wrong and tell them I said so!

Start laying the foundation now. "So, how do I lay the foundation?" you ask. It is quite simple. First, as I mentioned above you should find out everything you can about the career you have chosen using every resource you have available. Secondly, you need to begin interning in the *Real*

World. Work with your parents or teachers to arrange for you to go into various businesses to work for a day, week, month, or even the entire summer. You will get an inside look at what it is really like to work in that career. You can't get this experience in a classroom or from a textbook. You will see what you like and dislike. This is also called OJT – On the Job Training. You may even find a company that will have a job waiting for you when you graduate.

Success Versus Significance

There is richness in material gain or there is richness in people. Richness in material is the gain of "toys." The richness in people is the gain of relationships and friendship. Which do you prefer? I have experienced the people and the relationships; I have also experienced the acquiring of "toys" in my life. Which do I prefer? Having had both worlds, I will take the relationships and friendships any day over the "toys."

How do you define success? How do you define significance? Success is what others see, whereas significance is a result of the difference you have made and the feeling you have gained from making a difference. If you have to tell of your success, then you haven't really been a success and people aren't impressed. If someone else can tell of your success, then you gained the respect of others and have achieved significance.

Networking or Quilt-working

College will teach you that who you know plays a significant role in what you do or who you become. In some cases it's even about being in the right place at the right time. However, please let me add to this, as I have always thought more about Quilt-working then Networking.

Networking says, "Who is out there that has the resources I need and how do I get in contact with them?" Quilt-working says that there are many different pieces, colors, fabrics, patters, shapes, and sizes, and they all help to make the one piece we call a quilt. I have always lived my life believing that everyone is a part of the puzzle. The more people I get to meet and know, the more I grow, the more people I can help and the more people who can help me.

Networking says, "Who can help me?" where Quilt-working takes it a step further and says, "I need your help and I will help you and together we can reach our dreams." Everybody is a part of the puzzle of life. It doesn't matter if you are black or white, Jewish or Protestant, Catholic or Hindu, Latino or Asian. It doesn't matter if you go home and light candles, burn incense, throw salt over your shoulder and run around your house naked. The question is "Who are you working with, who do you trust, who can you help, who can you believe in and who believes in you?" Quilt-working begins where networking leaves off because quilt-working brings together individuals and makes them part of the puzzle.

The more people you know the further ahead you are. You meet people every day, but do you keep in contact with them?

Do you have an address book? Whether it is in your email or a $1.99 book you got from a local bookstore that stores addresses, use it. It is the most valuable $1.99 you'll ever spend in your life.

"Stay in touch with everyone FOREVER!
You never know where it can and will take you."
– Jeff Yalden

If you ask me what is the most important skill needed for anyone to become successful, without hesitation, I would reply communication. You communicate every day with people in every part of your life. This includes school, sports, business, and family situations, talking on the phone, emailing, instant messaging, and talking to a group. How well you communicate will determine people's perception of you, meaning how people think of you as a person.

Developing good communication skills as a teenager can make you "Super Successful" for the rest of your life. One of the key ingredients of successful communication skills is making contacts. The contacts you make every day will help you to succeed.

People are the shortcuts to success in the *Real World*. The more people you know, the more opportunities you will have and the richer your life will become.

Every person you build a relationship with for the rest of your life should be listed in your little $1.99 address book. Who you meet and what you talked about should all be listed in there and you should make a habit of keeping in touch with them at least once a year.

Get to know as many people as you can. Soon you'll need a more expensive address book, but it will be the best investment you'll ever make in your life. Before the car, fancy computers, nice offices, or clothes, buy that nice address book and make it your everything. Use it every day.

You never know who is influential, or who knows whom. In today's world, who you know can help you get ahead faster than anything else. Diversify your contacts by meeting different kinds of people (Quilt-working). Take the initiative to introduce yourself, start a conversation, and build a rapport with people.

Equally as important as meeting people is staying in touch. Meeting a person once will not help you in the future. You need to build a relationship, get their address and phone number, list them in your address book, then stay in touch forever with that person even when their address and phone number changes. No excuses.

One thing I do now in my business is write a newsletter monthly. I do this to keep in touch and to let people know where I am and what I have been up to. It is a way to continue the relationship. Perhaps, they may need a speaker in the future and someone has forwarded them my email. Maybe they forgot about me. Perhaps they visited my website and forgot that I am a speaker, but on a monthly basis they receive my newsletter by email. It is just a way to say hello on a monthly basis and to let them know I care about them.

You can send thank you notes, birthday cards, Christmas cards, Thanksgiving cards, anniversary cards, and just hello letters. Call them periodically and occasionally get together for a quick visit. Keep in touch.

Here is proof that this works ...

In 2003, I had the honor of speaking at the Florida State Student Council Associations Conference. I met a great lady who has become a friend whom I respect and admire. Her name is Carrie Coons. She is the executive director of Florida State Student Council and National Honor Society. There were a few times that I needed something and knew that she could lead me in the right direction.

Carrie and I were talking one day and she gave me the name of someone who is directly responsible and the executive director of the Southern Association of Student Council. Her name is Patti Ireland. Well, I wrote a little email and introduced myself to Patti and said I would be honored if she would pass my name along as a possible speaker for their next conference. As a result of Carrie and Patti knowing each other, I was selected to be one of the keynote speakers at the Southern Association of Student Council Conference in Humble, Texas. I had an awesome time and it resulted in my booking about four state conferences as a result, which in turn led to meeting more people, sharing new experiences and making my business grow.

Carrie is on my list to receive my newsletter and so is Patti Ireland. Just this past week, Carrie also sent an email to me about a lady in Michigan who is seeking a speaker for her advisors. I called right away and talked with her and gave Carrie's name as a point of contact about the success we had with her students.

Carrie, I love you. Let me know what I can do for you now.

Don't be afraid to introduce yourself to people, and stay in touch with everyone that you meet. This includes all teenage friends, high school friends, college friends, teachers, professors, sports teammates, business associates, your parents' friends, your relatives' friends, people you work with, people you work for – EVERYONE! You just never know where it could lead.

CHAPTER 8

Success and Money – The Bottom Line

You need to understand a few things about success and money. First, having money does not mean you are successful. Drug dealers have a lot of money, big homes, and drive some nice fancy cars. Does that mean they are successful? No! Success is much more than money.

One of the best definitions of success I have ever heard came from Legendary UCLA basketball coach John Wooden. Coach Wooden's definition of success is:

"Peace of mind which is a direct result of
self-satisfaction in knowing you did your
best to become the best that you are
capable of becoming."
– John Wooden

Success is all about feeling good about yourself as a result of what you do because you know that deep down inside you did your best and contributed to this wonderful world we live in. You made a difference. Success is about happiness – happiness within yourself and the life you lead.

There is nothing wrong with wanting to have money. The problem exists when you make money your main focus. You become greedy; your life becomes twisted and you become very selfish. If you work hard and do what makes you happy, then the money will follow.

Think about finding a career that is rewarding, meaningful, and fulfilling. Now think of doing that job and making average money. Compare that feeling to working a career you despise. You dread Monday mornings, the drive makes you sick, the people make your skin crawl, but yeah you are making great money. The weekend comes and what are you like? The difference between the two is that you can live happily within the money you make but all the money in the world can't make you happy. Work for the enjoyment of the job, not the money. Remember it's in the workplace that you'll spend most of your time. Why not make it a place that you enjoy?

Have you ever heard, "Money doesn't grow on trees?" Whoever said it was right. Since it doesn't grow on trees and doesn't come to us as often as we'd like, don't you think we should save what we have? Most teenagers and adults think that spending is a hobby, and that you can always squeeze an extra $20 out of your pocket or someone else's. I have news for you: Other people will not always be there to play Mr. and Mrs. Bank Teller. There will come a time in the very near future when you will be responsible for earning and managing your own money. You will soon find out that spending is not as much fun when it's your own money. It's time to learn some basic principles of good money management.

Saving Money

Saving money means that you don't spend it. That is right, no spending! By this I mean no more $120 sneakers, no more $100 CD player, no more $60 jeans, and no more $50 concert tickets. Don't let your peers spend your money! The idea of saving is to keep more than you spend. The more you can save now, the more you will have later.

The problem is most teenagers don't have much self-control when it comes to saving money. Listed below are a few tips that will help you to save, at least a portion of what you have.

1. Put a portion of any money you earn from working in a savings account at a bank. Ask your parents or an adult to help you open your own account.

2. Be a smart shopper. Do not just buy things for the fun of it. Buy only what is necessary. ($120 basketball sneakers when you can only play $1.99 worth of basketball is not necessary.)

3. Leave your money at home when going to the mall or to stores. You are more likely to spend money when in the mall or stores. You can always go home to get money if there is something you absolutely must buy.

4. Follow the "Golden Rule" to becoming wealthy. Take 10% of anything you earn and put if away forever. This means that you never touch it unless it's an

extreme emergency (buying a new game for Sony Play station is not an emergency). If you continue to put 10% away from every paycheck for the next 20-30 years you will become very wealthy.

(I highly suggest the book *The Wealthy Barber* for all teenagers and young adults.)

Credit Cards

I remember when I received my first credit card. I immediately ran to K-Mart and bought stuff for my office. I had no computer, but I had a desk and now I had files, paper, a stapler, a hole puncher, pens, pencils, books, calendars, etc. Pretty soon the credit cards kept coming, and so did the nice computer. This was awesome. I had a nice office; little did I know that I had to pay it all back. To make matters worse, I was charged interest. This meant I would repay more than the money I spent. (Ouch!)

Also, when you get a credit card at 9% interest, please read the details and fine print. Just send in one payment late and that 9% increases to about 19-21% interest without them even telling you ahead of time and YES they can do that.

Charging items on a credit card is like taking a loan from a bank. It must be repaid, with interest. It's not free money and could get you in serious financial trouble if you go on a spending spree. Listed below are a few tips to help you avoid financial destruction:

1. Only charge what you know you can pay off when the monthly bill arrives. Never charge your card to the maximum limit. The higher your balance the less

money from your payment goes to paying off what you "borrowed." Most of it will go towards paying off the interest you owe on your loan.

2. Keep the receipts from all purchases so you can keep track of how much you have charged.

3. If you can't pay cash for it you probably don't need it.

Remember, credit is not free money. It is money you must repay, plus interest. The best way to use a credit card is not to use it and store it for emergency situations.

Investing

This simply means to put money into stocks, companies, 401 K's, IRA's, businesses, etc. in order to get a profit. When you invest, you are putting your money into something that you believe will grow your original investment and make you money. If it grows, you will receive more money back than you originally put into it. This is what investing is all about.

One of the most common ways to invest is to purchase stocks of companies. The way to buy stocks is through a stockbroker. Buying a few shares of stocks at a young age is one of the best ways to get started learning about investing and the stock market. A good way to begin investing is to buy stocks of companies whose products or services you already use. The following are a few examples:

McDonalds	Microsoft	Reebok
Burger King	Dell	Nike
Coca-Cola	Apple	IBM
PepsiCo	Disney	Sony

Ask yourself which products or services you and your friends use, then find out information on those companies. It may be worth buying a few shares if there is demand for their products or services. If you can't afford to buy the stocks try investing without spending any money. Pick some stocks, write down the number of shares and the price you would have paid. Then follow their progress over weeks and months to see how well you've done. You'll learn many valuable lessons and the best thing is all you have to "spend" is your time.

Another investment vehicle is stock mutual funds. A stock mutual fund is like an Easter egg basket filled with eggs. The basket is the mutual fund and the eggs are the individual stocks. When you buy a mutual fund you own a piece of the stocks in your basket. How well the stocks do in the fund determines how well the overall fund performs. Mutual funds are a good way to diversity your risk because you own pieces of many stocks rather than just buying one stock. Some mutual fund companies will allow you to start investing with as little as $50 to $100.

How to Become a Millionaire

Forget about "Get-Rich-Quick" schemes. The best way to create wealth is by investing for the long term. The key is to start early.

If you are working as a teenager, great! If you are not, then you may want to consider getting a job so you can earn a little money to invest. Think about it. If you are like most teenagers, you probably live at home with your parents and have no bills or financial obligations. If you were to get a part-time job, you could earn enough to invest and begin creating your fortune. Consider the following example:

Suppose you were to get a part-time job and worked only 15 hours per week and got paid $5 per hour. You would earn $75 per week. That's $300 per month and $3,600 per year. Let's suppose that $600 of the $3,600 you earn a year is what you owe to Uncle Sam for income tax. That would leave you with $3,000.

Since you are working and have earned income, you can invest up to $2,000 a year in an Individual Retirement Account (IRA). An IRA is an account that allows you to put money into it to be used for your retirement. You do not pay any taxes on the growth of the money until it is withdrawn, usually between the ages of 60-65.

If you invest $2,000 a year from age 15 to 19 and never invest any more after age 19, (assuming your annual return of at least 12%) your money would be worth more than $1,000,000 by age 59 1/2. Dude, that is AWESOME!

Compounding interest creates a huge snowball effect. Your interest keeps accumulating over the years without losing a portion of your growth to income taxes.

If you withdraw any portion of your money before age 59 1/2, there is a 10% penalty on any money taken out and it is also subject to income tax.

If you take $2,000 of the $3,000 you earn from your part-time job and invest it in an IRA, and you do that from age 15 to 19 (5 years), you will become a millionaire. The following table illustrates how your money would grow.

Age	Year	Investment	15%	14%
15	1	$2,000	$2,300	$2,280
16	2	$2,000	$4,945	$4,879
17	3	$2,000	$7,987	$7,842
18	4	$2,000	$11,485	$11,220
19	5	$2,000	$15,507	$15,071
20	6	0	$17,834	$17181
30	16	0	$72,147	$63,694
40	26	0	$291,874	$236,127
50	36	0	$1,180,794	$875,374
59	45	0	$4,153,888	$2,846,668

Age	Year	Investment	13%	12%
15	1	$2,000	$2,260	$2,240
16	2	$2,000	$4,814	$4,749
17	3	$2,000	$7,700	$7,559
18	4	$2,000	$10,961	$10,706
19	5	$2,000	$14,645	$14,230
20	6	0	$16,549	$15,938
30	16	0	$56,176	$49,501
40	26	0	$190,696	$153,743
50	36	0	$647,328	$477,502
59	45	0	$1,944,602	$1,324,150

(The author is only offering ideas and suggestions for investing. He is not promising or guaranteeing any investment returns or performance and is not liable for any losses that may occur to your investments. Consult your parents or a licensed financial advisor before starting any investing.)

The bottom line is to start saving at an early age and find someone who you trust and opinions you value. Start with buying a little stock, or investing in an IRA. Put away the money now at an early age and then you are set for life.

This chart on page 86 will show you how the money makes money from itself. The money keeps on compounding (making more money) even after you stop investing your own. The money will continue to grow. It may not grow on trees, but it will grow just the same.

CHAPTER 9

Never Stop Learning

"Education is the only thing you have left after you have forgotten everything you have learned."

– Jeff Yalden

Y ou have likely heard the phrase *Knowledge is Power!* How true this is. The more you learn, the more you grow. The more you grow, the more diverse your background becomes. The more diverse your background becomes, the more valuable you will be. Therefore, you will have more opportunities.

The problem with most people is they think they know it all. People who know it all are stopping themselves from learning. When you think you know it all, your mind isn't open to new ideas and opinions. They stagnate. They tell the same lame stories and they'll have the same skills 20 years from now as they do today.

When you open your mind to new ideas and opinions, you become more interesting. Make it a point to learn something new every day, whether in or out of school.

It's not only important to pay attention in school, but also outside of school. Pay attention to current events that are happening in everyday life. Take the initiative to keep learning.

Did you know that if you stay on top of current events every day you can hold yourself in an enjoyable conversation with anyone? You are bound to find something in common if you just keep learning. You'll be surprised at how much you know. Knowledge is not only power but it gives you self confidence and allows you to meet and talk to more people than you could ever imagine.

How do you keep learning though? It is very easy. Communicate and listen, write, read, and watch TV. Listen to talk shows on the radio instead of listening to music. Let's take some time and start with communicating and listening since they go hand in hand.

Communicate and Listen

"We have two ears and one mouth.
We should listen more than we talk."
– Jeff Yalden

Every day of your life you find yourself communicating. Every time you communicate with someone you have the opportunity to learn something new if you just take the time to listen. Most people communicate and never listen. They want to talk and get their own opinions out rather than listen to the opinions of others. Talk to a variety of people – people of different ages, nationalities, and backgrounds. Don't be intimidated because they may be a little different than you.

It's easy to get people talking. Simply ask them questions. People love talking about themselves, especially if they feel they are teaching you how to do something. It makes them feel important. Questions always can start a conversation and they are the key to keeping it going. Never be afraid to ask people questions because you believe they'll think less of you. Asking questions is how they learned and it's how you'll learn and gain knowledge.

Writing

Another great way to learn is by writing. This includes letters, research papers, and even a book! One of my favorite exercises that I have teenagers do in my seminars is called the "Learn about Myself" exercise. Try it; you'll be amazed at what you will learn about yourself. Write the following on a piece of paper, and then answer them honestly.

1. Which five things do I most value in my life?

2. Which five goals are most important to me?

3. Who are the five most important people in my life?

4. What would I do if I won $1,000,000 today?

5. What would I do if I only had 6 months to live?

6. Which one thing would I try if I knew I could not fail?

7. Which one thing would I change about the world?

After the completion of the questions I then ask this:

If 24 hours, 7 days a week I see you, but you can't see me, what would I see you doing that shows that you place a value on any of your answers listed above?

You don't need to show your answers to anyone. The exercise is to help you learn about yourself. Do this exercise at least once a year. Your answers will probably change every year as you mature.

Here is another exercise that I love. Take a few pieces of paper or a journal and write at the top: "Who am I? & What do I want?" Now, for 30 minutes write non-stop your answers to these two questions.

At the end of the 30 minutes, reread what you wrote and take out any negative answers. Get another piece of paper. On this sheet of paper, turn the negative answers into positives and rework the questions from Why to How. An example is as follows:

If you wrote, "I am negative and too selfish," turn the questions from "Why am I like this?" to "How can I make this a positive characteristic trait about myself?"

For example, "How can I become more positive and unselfish?" Now you have asked a better question and it is up to you to take personal responsibility to make the change.

The difference here is that "why" questions leave you blaming the circumstances around you and not taking personal responsibility. "How" questions get you to take personal responsibility and to come up with the answers and take action.

Value Card

Here is the quickest way to raise your self-esteem. Get an index card. On the top of it write "Value Card." List five things on it that you value. It could be family, faith, friends, education, money, cars, etc. What do you value? There is no right or wrong. They are your values and nobody can take that away from you. As you get older your values will change as you mature. Here is my personal value card.

My Value Card:

1. Faith (My relationship with my Higher Power)

2. Family & Friends (It's fine to put them together)

3. Education (Always be learning)

4. Fitness & Health

5. Time

Now you can take this a step further. After every value write a paragraph for WHY you value that. Here is an example of mine:

My Value Card:

– Faith (My relationship with my Higher Power)

- I thank my Higher Power for the ability to do what I do and for the love I have in my life. Without His support, energy, enthusiasm, and love I wouldn't be who I am today. He uses me to reach my audience. He works through me to speak to you.

– Family & Friends (It's fine to put them together)

- Family provided me with support, food, clothing, and the wisdom to start my life. Friends are there for encouragement, support, listening, and communicating. I get love from both family and friends and that is very important in self-esteem.

- Education (Always be learning)
  - Education is the only thing I have left after I have forgotten everything I have learned. Seek every day to be smarter and more knowledgeable than I was the day before.

- Fitness & Health
  - If I am not in shape, I am not In-Purpose. Eat right for energy. Eat to live; don't live to eat.

- Time
  - My time is limited so I appreciate every moment I have. Time is sensitive, fragile, and limited. Take advantage of the little time I have to maximize everything I can out of it.

Reading

The first thing I would suggest is to read the newspaper every day to stay informed about current events. Remember, by you staying on top of current events you can hold your own in any conversation, intellectual or otherwise, with anyone.

You never know when you are going to be put into a position where you will need to discuss a current event. If you only focus on reading one part of the paper, it could make you feel uncomfortable in certain situations. So read the sports section and the headlines, your local news and world events.

Read books on self-help; read articles in a magazine. It's been proven that you can increase your knowledge and even your vocabulary simply by reading. Keep a dictionary nearby when you read. If you don't understand a word, don't just breeze by it. Take a minute to look it up and understand the definition. You will be learning a new word. Also, when speaking with someone and they use a word you are not familiar with, don't be afraid to ask what that word means. They will be impressed that you asked and you will also learn a new word.

Watching TV

Have your parents ever complained to you that you watch too much television? They're not entirely wrong. Television is okay if you watch it in moderation and give yourself a time limit of what to watch. You don't want to waste your life by becoming a couch potato eating potato chips and drinking soda.

Television is great if you can learn from what you are watching. I'm not saying you shouldn't watch the no-nonsense sitcoms. Hey, I love *Will & Grace, Friends, Everybody Loves Raymond,* and Sports.

What I am simply saying is that there are certain times when watching the television to learn is okay. Just as you read the newspaper to keep up on current events, you should also watch the local or world news. It only takes 30 minutes of local news to get updated on the most important stories.

Try not to watch anything negative before you go to bed. What goes in as you close your eyes at night also wakes up with you when you open your eyes in the morning. So watch something positive and happy so that you wake up positive and happy.

In addition to the news, there are other quality programs that can serve as informative and as educational outlets, such as PBS and the Discovery Channel. I also think ESPN is informative to keep updated in the world of sports.

I am not telling you not to watch movies either. I am a big fan of some great movies. There are some great movies out there that everyone can learn from. Here are two that can teach you some important success principles:

Rocky I & II

Remember when Sylvester Stallone played boxer Rocky Balboa and he had the chance to fight Apollo Creed for the World Heavyweight Boxing title? No one gave him a chance. But no matter how bad Rocky was beaten up or how many times he was knocked down in the fight, he kept getting up. In Rocky II, he became the Heavyweight Champion and proved that you can accomplish your dreams if you simply "go for it" and keep getting up when you're knocked down.

Rudy

This is a story of a student who didn't have the grades to get into his dream school, The University of Notre Dame. After going to another school and improving his grades his dream came true. The University of Notre Dame accepted him. Then he tried out for the football team. His dream was to play one play in a real game, but he was much smaller than the other players and not as athletic. He never lost focus of his dream. Finally, he got the chance to play, sacked the quarterback, and at the end of the game, he was carried off the field on the shoulders of his teammates. No other player since "Rudy" has ever been carried off the field at the University of Notre Dame. It's a great movie about pursuing your dreams and not quitting.

Chapter 10

If Not You – WHO?

You have to believe in yourself regardless of any circumstances, past happenings, family backgrounds, adversities, etc. The belief in oneself is the most important habit you can learn to adopt. As you journey through life you will meet people who tell you that you're not smart enough to succeed. You will meet people who tell you that you don't have the ability to succeed. And you will certainly meet people who just don't believe in you or your abilities. So if you don't believe in yourself and the dreams you desire, then who will?

Condition Your Mind

You can't achieve anything unless you first believe it. Condition your mind to believe that you WILL achieve your dreams.

Your brain is a muscle. Like any other muscle in your body, it needs to be exercised in order for it to grow, become stronger, and increase its performance. The way to accomplish this is through proper exercise of your muscle (brain). Like any other muscle, stop using it and you lose it.

Bill Gates is the richest man in America with an estimated net worth of about $50 billion dollars. (That's right, *billion!*) He is the founder and president of Microsoft. You have undoubtedly used computer software designed by his company, Microsoft.

In a recent interview, Bill was asked how he is able to develop unique ideas and concepts that continuously put Microsoft ahead of all other computer software companies. His answer was amazing, yet very simple.

Bill Gates told a story of his childhood. He said that one day his mother could not find him anywhere in the house. Finally, she opened the closet door and found him sitting there in the dark closet. When his mother asked him why he was sitting in a dark closed, he replied, "I'm thinking."

Bill went on in the interview to stress how important it is to exercise your brain because it responds to repetitive exercise.

I like the quote that says, "Repetition is the mother of skill," meaning that in order for you to improve or increase performance, you need to practice the fundamentals over and over again.

Studies have indicated that it takes approximately 21-30 days to create a new habit. This means that if you want to change or create a belief in your mind, it should become a natural habit after working on it for 21-30 days.

"We are what we repeatedly do.
Excellence then, is not an act, but a habit."
– Aristotle

Rights & Privileges Versus Responsibilities & Obligations

It was April of 2003. I was speaking at a youth conference in Utah when a bunch of state police officers surrounded me after my program. My first response was, "Oh no! I'm caught; they got me." Then I realized I didn't do anything. They asked me a question that I will never forget. They asked me what I thought was the difference between today's youth and youth of 20 years ago. I thought long and hard and replied, "I think today's young people are thinking about their rights and privileges when twenty years ago they were thinking about their responsibilities and obligations."

What I am trying to say is simply this: You want and think you deserve rights and certain privileges, and I agree. However, rights and privileges are earned as a result of one characteristic trait called TRUST. When people trust you they tend to give you more rights and privileges. Therefore, you need to understand that once you fulfill your responsibilities and obligations, then your rights and privileges will be greater. Does that make sense? Do what you're supposed to do, when you should be doing it, at the time you should be doing it and people will trust you; therefore, you will gain greater rights and privileges. Don't ever overlook the simple understanding that it's the responsibilities and obligations that give you the opportunity to earn more rights and privileges.

I decided at a young age that my intelligence and ability were not going to get me the great success and significance I wanted, nor that I thought I deserved. Therefore, I chose to dedicate my life to hard work. I knew there were people who were a lot smarter than me. I knew there were people who were better athletically, more gifted academically, and more suited intellectually. However, I wasn't going to let someone out-work me. I was committed to being more prepared and hungry in going after what I wanted to achieve what I thought I deserved.

Today, I live a great life as a simple result to my commitment to work hard and not let anyone out-work me. I take great pride in my work ethic and credit my family's ethic rubbing off on me.

The thrill of achieving your goals and dreams is knowing that you put in the time and worked hard for it. Whether it is receiving an "A" in school, getting an academic or athletic scholarship, landing a great job, earning a million dollars, helping a charity, or whatever, the satisfaction of knowing that it was your dedication, your commitment, and your effort is what makes achieving a goal worthwhile.

Let me also say this: I didn't do well in school. I scored a 680 and a 610 on my SATs. I grew up with a learning disability, but now I realize that I just learn differently. I graduated 128 out of 133 students. I always thought I was stupid and didn't have the ability. I realize now that I didn't commit to being the best and working hard at an early age. My point is simply this: Work hard and commit to being the best you can. Whether you get an "A" a "B" or maybe even a "C" doesn't matter. Just do the best you can. If you did the best you can and a "B" or "C" is the best you can do, then you should be proud.

Every night when you lay your head on the pillow, ask yourself this question: "Did I give today my very best?" Also ask: "Am I a better person today than I was yesterday as a result of my hard work?" That is what I am talking about. If you aren't committed to working hard then you aren't committed to succeeding in what you do.

Commit yourself to working harder than everyone you know. Don't let them out-work you. They might be more gifted, may have more money, nicer clothes, nicer car, but a work ethic and commitment to excellence comes from within your heart and soul. I promise you that if you commit to working hard you'll achieve what you want and more.

CHAPTER 11

Be Grateful

One of the best exercises I have ever done is the Grateful Journal I keep. Every day, I write down five things I am grateful for, and no day can be a repeat of the day before. Every single day is a new day and a day to come up with five new things to be grateful for. Try it. It's hard after a while. However, it really teaches you to appreciate the little things in life. Here's an example:

Grateful Journal (date)

1. My Freedom
2. My Friends
3. Financial Success
4. Airplane Travel
5. My Family

Then you do another day. Remember, this new day has to have a completely new list. Nothing identical.

This little piece of work has taught me many things, including a simple appreciation for our everyday existence in a world that is second to none. I mean, every day, I stop and think about how grateful I am to travel and work with youth. I am grateful that I can get on a plane at 3 p.m. on the east coast and be doing a 7:30 a.m. school assembly in San Francisco.

When was the last time you stopped to think about our ability to travel so easily? How about the opportunity to just see different cultures, meet new people, see different life styles, and frequent great parts of the country?

I have learned what's really important in life – faith, good health, family, and friends. We take all this for granted way too much. How about personal safety? I travel close to 250,000 miles a year. I go from flight to rental car to hotel. I wake up and speak and do it all over again. The fact that I have not had any major challenges, accidents, delays, etc. is just a total miracle. I am grateful for this. How about just the ability to pursue your dreams? You have the ability and so does everyone, but how many people are afraid to pursue the dream? Many!

Take a minute to think about who is important in your life, and then tell them that you love them and care about them. Be thankful for what you have. You may wake up one day and have a piece of it missing.

Appreciate Your Parents and Loved Ones

How many times have you complained that your parents or guardians are getting on your case or being too nosey? Have you ever said you can't stand them and can't wait until you no longer live in their house?

Think about something. Why do you think that they wait up for you when you're out late? Why do they tell you to be home at a certain time? It's not because they're on your case. It's because they love and care about you.

The next time your parents or guardians are waiting up for you or tell you to be home at a certain time, thank them. Tell them that you appreciate the fact that they care about you enough to worry.

I have never met one person in my entire life who doesn't want to be cared for and loved. Imagine if no one cared. Many teenagers in the world don't have loving parents or guardians. Many teenagers are beaten daily, sexually abused, and physically and emotionally scarred for life.

Appreciate your parents and loved ones. Tell them that you love, respect, and care about them. The problem with most teenagers is that they take their parents and those who care about them for granted. They don't realize what their loved ones may have sacrificed and done for them throughout the years.

Stop reading this book now. Don't read any further to-day. Just put the book away and sit back and think about all the little things that your loved ones have sacrificed for you. How have they gone out of their way to help you? Show them you appreciate them by telling them "thank you" and that you love them. Do it now. You never know what may happen tomorrow. They may not be around.

CHAPTER 12

The Conclusion of a Great Life

My life today is rich with love and made meaningful through the support and testimonials from people who have heard my message. My life is fulfilling, challenging, rewarding, and a journey of happiness and giving. I have the greatest job in the world. Every year over one million students and teachers hear and benefit from my message.

I have a beautiful wife, Marsha, who has been there with love, support, encouragement, and sanity. Along with my wife, I have many friends and family members that are incredibly dear to me. To me this is special. I couldn't be who I am today if it weren't for the support and love of those around me. I am so thankful to all the people that have been there along the way and have helped me reach the position I am in now. I have realized one cannot do it alone.

If you invest in helping others reach their dreams, then people will invest in helping you reach yours. This may have taken me time to learn but, as I have learned, it was well worth the wait in the end. All my life I wanted to be successful. Not really knowing what success was, I just wanted it. It was all about me and what I wanted: money and financial freedom. I knew exactly what I wanted to earn in terms of dollars, the house I would live in, and the car I would drive. I wanted to make a nice living. What is a nice living? I can tell you this, ladies and gentleman: The moment my attitude changed and I was less concerned with making a living and I started to concentrate more on making a difference, I made a much more significant living.

The Journey Is What We Miss, But It's What Life Is Really About

Success is the journey and not the destination. One's true success is the significance felt when helping other people achieve what they want in life. Significance is a personal feeling of living a life that has made a difference in the lives of other people. I wish you many titles and testimonials throughout your life, but I am sure you will find true satisfaction comes from testimonies rather than titles.

I am successful because I am on a journey that I have set and created. I am doing what I love and journeying towards my goals and dreams. I am significant because I am reaching out to help others by making them feel special and good about themselves. I receive letters and emails from those who have really been touched by my words. Those letters and emails are testimonies of my significance.

I think significance is far more important than financial success. I really think it is about helping others before helping oneself. I wish you greatness in life and lots of titles, successes, testimonies, and significance. But, if you had to choose between them, go for testimonies and significance. If you do, you will find life to be extremely rewarding and fulfilling, meaningful, and significant. Good luck and God Bless.

I personally hope that you have enjoyed reading this book as much as I have enjoyed writing it for you. Bye!

The Last Word

One of the greatest things we can do in the world is learning to help others. It is the best feeling in the world to know that you have made a difference in someone's life by helping them. That's what the world and our society should be about, helping others, especially the less fortunate.

I have listed here what I think are some things you should keep in mind in order to be a good person:

- Listen more than you talk.
- Be on time.
- Be grateful.
- Help others without expecting anything in return.
- Express your interest in others.
- Be honest.
- Open the door for other people.
- Say hello with a smile.
- Put other people's needs before your own needs.
- Respect all people.

Success Planner

Think You Can

What do you personally believe about yourself?

_____

_____

_____

_____

How does this affect your behaviors? (Be Specific)

_____

_____

_____

_____

What can you do TODAY to change your beliefs? How do you think that will affect your behaviors?

_____

_____

_____

_____

Your Attitude Is Everything

Define your new attitude:

_____

_____

_____

_____

How do you think your attitude affects your everyday life?

_____

_____

_____

_____

What are you going to do when you notice your attitude is becoming negative?

_____

_____

_____

Why are you special?

_____

_____

_____

List five failures you have had in your life. Did you quit or persevere? If you could go back now and replay what happened, what would you do differently?

_____

_____

_____

_____

_____

_____

_____

Who are five role models in your life? Do you learn from their wisdom and experiences? Can you ask them better and more questions?

_____

_____

_____

_____

_____

_____

_____

_____

Two Types of People in the World

What makes you In-Purpose?

_____

_____

_____

_____

What makes you Out-of-Purpose?

_____

_____

_____

_____

Have Commitments In Life

What are your commitments?

_____

_____

_____

_____

What are you going to take personal responsibility of now?

_____

_____

_____

How can the 4 T's help you in your personal life?

_____

_____

_____

_____

Where in your life can you do better?

_____

_____

_____

_____

How can you treat people better in your life?

_____

_____

_____

_____

Say No to Drugs

How have drugs affected your life?

_____

_____

_____

_____

When do you feel the need to be accepted by other students?

_____

_____

_____

_____

What can you do now to not feel the need to be accepted by others?

_____

_____

_____

_____

What role does alcohol play in your future successes?

_____

_____

_____

_____

What is another example of negative influences in your life?

_____

_____

_____

_____

Write Down Your Goals

List your one-year goals.

_____

_____

_____

List your three-year goals.

_____

_____

_____

_____

List your five-year goals.

_____

_____

_____

_____

SMART (Specific, Measurable, Attainable, Reasonable, and Timely) – Describe how this helps you to define your goals further?

_____

_____

_____

_____

Describe your Purpose versus your Goals?

_____

_____

_____

_____

Plan for the Future

Where do you want to go to college or what branch of the military do you want to join?

_____

_____

List four majors you have an interest in.

_____

_____

_____

_____

What jobs interest you for a career choice where you would support a family and enjoy life?

_____

_____

_____

_____

How can you find out more information about this specific career opportunity?

_____

_____

Describe the difference between Success and Significance? Describe in terms of people you know. What does it mean to you?

_____

_____

Success and Money

How much money would you like to earn? What do you think it will take to earn that kind of money?

_____

_____

Your rent/mortgage will cost? _____

Your car payment will cost? _____

Your monthly food will cost? _____

Your monthly utilities:

      Electricity _____

      Telephone _____

      Cell _____

      Television _____

Monthly Entertainment _____

Taxes are 33% of your income which is _____

TOTAL MONTHLY EXPENSES _____

Save 10% = _____

What is left for you? _____

Is that enough money to live the life you want?

_____

_____

_____

_____

What can you do today to ensure that you have done everything to prepare for your future?

_____

_____

_____

_____

What do credit cards mean to you?

_____

_____

_____

_____

How many credit cards do you think you should carry?

_____

_____

_____

_____

Seek the Wisdom of Others

Who in your life do you respect, trust, and admire?

_____

_____

_____

_____

What wisdom do they have that can benefit you as a person?

_____

_____

_____

_____

Fundamentals in Life

What do fundamentals mean to you?

_____

_____

_____

_____

How do you benefit as a result of fundamentals?

_____

_____

_____

What are your responsibilities?

_____

_____

_____

_____

Networking and Quilt-working

Who has resources that I can use?

_____

_____

_____

_____

Investing

Three books that I am going to read for investing?

_____

_____

_____

Who in my family knows about money and investing that I can talk to?

_____

_____

_____

Grateful Journal

What are five things I am grateful for today?

_____

_____

_____

_____

_____

_____

_____

_____

_____

Appreciate your Parents

How can I show better appreciation towards my parents?

_____

_____

_____

_____

_____

_____

_____

_____

About the Author

J eff Yalden is one of the most sought after youth speakers in education today. He has addressed hundreds of youth conferences, thousands of middle schools, high schools, colleges and universities. His wisdom and unparalleled ability to reach into the hearts of his audience have enabled him to share his message with audiences in 48 states and five countries. Since 1995, Jeff Yalden has been speaking professionally and has addressed over 2.5 million youth and educators.

He is a distinguished member of the National Speakers Association, International Speakers Association, and New England Speakers Association. Jeff has earned the designation of Certified Speaking Professional, a designation earned by less that 3% of all professional speakers world-wide. Along with his success speaking, Jeff Yalden was also two-time Marine of the Year and Mr. New Hampshire Male America.

In addition to the current book, Jeff is the author of *Keep It Simple, 20 Ways to Keep It Simple,* and *Traits of a Leader*. He is the co-author of *Lead Now or Step Aside* and contributing author to the *New York Times* #1 best-seller, *A Cup of Chicken Soup for the Soul*.

From his past to his present, Jeff has lived his message making it more real and entertaining. As a student in high school, Jeff graduated 128 out of 133 students. He was rejected by 16 of the 19 colleges that he applied to. Having grown up with a learning disability, stutter, ADD and ADHD, Jeff had to struggle and fight hard to overcome obstacles.

When Jeff is not on the road inspiring young and old alike, he resides in southern New Hampshire with his wife Marsha and their chocolate lab, Chase and cat, Tasha.

CONTACT JEFF TODAY
FOR YOUR NEXT YOUTH EVENT

Programs are available for:

Middle Schools

High Schools

Colleges

Universities

Youth Leadership Conferences

· Church Programs

Teacher In-Services

Parent/Community Programs

Corporate Events

Commencement Addresses

For information about Jeff
and his programs please visit:

www.JeffYalden.com

or call today
Toll Free 1-800-948-9289

Quick Order Form

Fax: (603) 878-4215 (*send this form or a copy of this form*)

Call: (800) 948-9289

Web: www.jeffyalden.com

Write: Jeff Yalden, CSP
PO Box 541, Greenville, NH 03048

❑ Please send me ___ copies of *Pathway to Purpose* at $12.95 each, plus shipping and handling.

Name: _____ Date: _____

Address: _____

City: _____ State: _____ Zip: _____

Phone: _____ Email: _____

Shipping: US: $3 for the first book and $2 for each additional book.

International: Based on ship-to location and current rates; please call for exact amounts.

Payment type: ❑ Credit Card   ❑ Check/Money Order
❑ Visa   ❑ Mastercard   ❑ American Express

Credit card #: _____

Name on card: _____ exp date: _____

Signature: _____

Marik
Hirsch